Action Safety

Written by Sharon Parsons

Contents Page

Chapter 1. *Speedier and Speedier* 4

Chapter 2. *Sudden Stops* 8

Chapter 3. *Crashes and Crumples* 14

Chapter 4. *Escape!* 18

Special Feature: *Meet A Flight Team Pilot!* 22

Chapter 5. *Extreme Sports* 24

Chapter 6. *Speedy Fun* 28

Index And Bookweb Links 32

Glossary Inside Back Cover

Rigby

Chapter Snapshots

1. Speedier and Speedier   Page 4

People have always wanted to go faster!
While race cars can travel at speeds of more than
200 miles an hour, drivers need protection in
case something goes wrong!

2. Sudden Stops   Page 8

Every car is designed with safety in mind.
Luckily, there are plenty of dummies to test that
the design and safety features work!

3. Crashes and Crumples   Page 14

Accidents can happen on two wheels as well as
on four wheels! And with bicycles and
motorbikes, there's not much between riders
and the ground!

"A flashing red ligh

4. Escape! Page 18

Whether people are
flying in aircraft
or sailing at sea,
they need
safety equipment
to protect them from
danger. And, to escape
if something goes wrong!

5. Extreme Sports Page 24

Some sports are so fast and action-packed,
they need their own kind of safety protection!

6. Speedy Fun Page 28

Bumper cars, in-line skates, and
playing in swimming pools —
even when we're having fun, people have
already thought about how to keep us safe!

varns you of danger."

1. Speedier And Speedier

Imagine this ...

You are a race car driver, speeding around
a race track at almost 150 miles an hour.
As you speed around the bend, your car skids.

Suddenly, you feel a wobble in your steering wheel. Your car's front right tire has split. You can't steer the car. Your car is zooming toward the crash barrier!

As your car hits the crash barrier, the safety technology in your car, your helmet, and your safety clothes could save your life.

The Need for Speed

Ever since people first used motor vehicles for transportation, they have wanted to travel faster and faster. The first cars could only travel at 10 miles an hour. Today, race cars can travel at more than 200 miles an hour! As cars have become faster, we have found better ways of protecting people.

Drag Racing

Drag race drivers wear special clothes to protect themselves. They also use a parachute to help slow them down! The parachute catches the wind and pulls the car to a stop. The fastest speed that a drag racing car has reached is 324 miles an hour. Lucky it had a parachute!

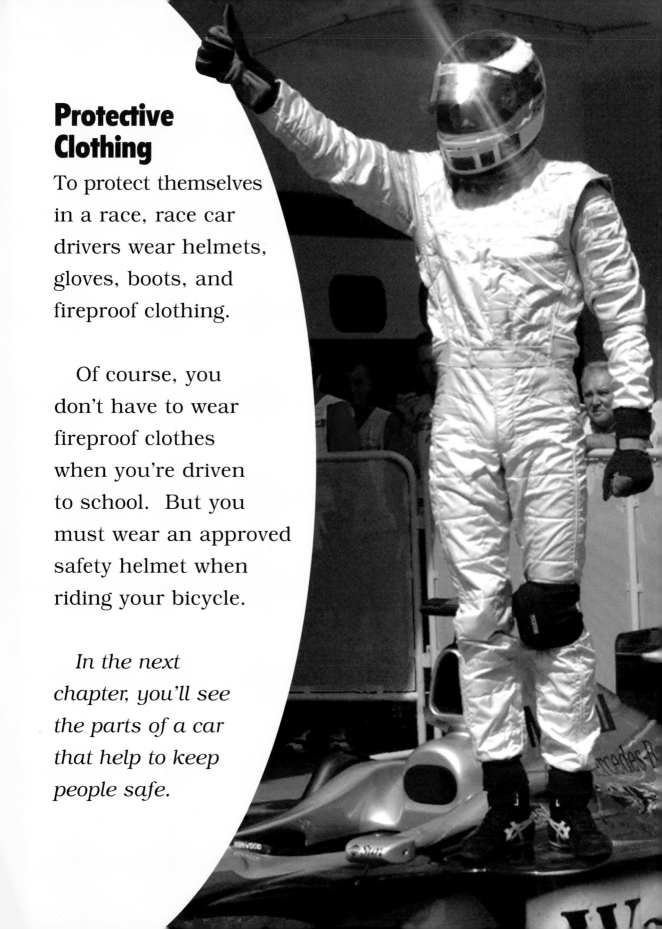

Protective Clothing

To protect themselves in a race, race car drivers wear helmets, gloves, boots, and fireproof clothing.

Of course, you don't have to wear fireproof clothes when you're driven to school. But you must wear an approved safety helmet when riding your bicycle.

In the next chapter, you'll see the parts of a car that help to keep people safe.

2. Sudden Stops

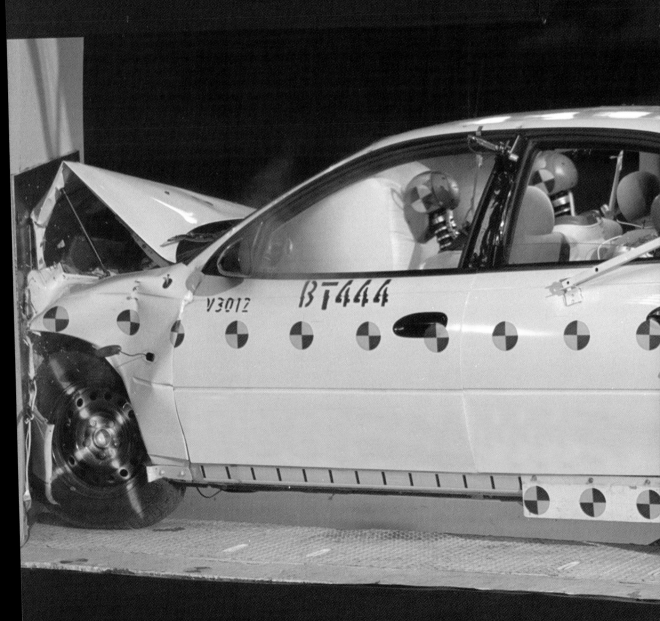

Imagine this ...

In this car safety test, the car is traveling at 60 miles an hour. The dummy driver and passengers will move forward at 60 miles an hour when the car hits the wall. How are the dummies protected?

Safety Tests

Carmakers test their cars to make sure they are built safely. A video camera records what happens during the car safety test. This helps companies build safer cars for us to travel in.

Seat Belts

Seat belts in motor vehicles, such as cars and trucks, have saved millions of lives. All drivers and passengers must wear seat belts. Seat belts hold people in a safe position if the vehicle stops suddenly. They stop people from moving forward and maybe hurting themselves.

How Seat Belts Work

A seat belt has a small wheel that allows us to pull the seat belt around our body. The wheel also locks into place if the seat belt is tugged quickly. If the vehicle stops suddenly and we move forward quickly, the seat belt holds us safely in our seat.

Child Safety Seats

Babies and small children could slip through the

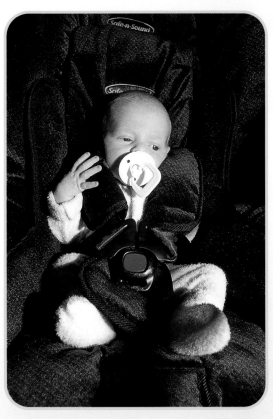

straps of a seat belt. So they sit in special child safety seats. The seat is fixed to the car's seat belt anchor so it doesn't move if the car stops suddenly. The special shape of the safety seat also stops a small child from rolling or falling sideways in an accident.

Brakes

Brakes can prevent us from having an accident. For cars, trucks, motorcycles, and bicycles, brakes are used to slow the wheels down and stop.

Brakes work by pressing onto the wheels and slowing them down. In motor vehicles, all we have to do is press the brake pedal to make the brakes work.

When we use the brakes, red brake lights flash on at the back of the vehicle. The lights tell the driver behind us to slow down, too.

Air Bags

In many cars, air bags are hidden in the steering wheel and dashboard. In an accident, the air bags will quickly burst out and fill with air. The air bag acts as a soft cushion between us and the hard parts of the car.

Inside the frame of this car is a high-tech dummy. The dummy is specially made to help car companies test the steel frames of new cars.

Steel Frames

Cars and trucks are built with strong steel frames. One main purpose for the steel frames is to protect people in an accident.

Safety on the Outside

On the outside of the steel frame, many materials are used to help keep us safe, such as:

1. plastic and metal bumpers

2. very strong metal and glass

3. Crashes and Crumples

Riding Safely

Motorcycle riders wear special clothing to protect themselves in an accident. Safety technology can save their lives. Their helmets, gloves, boots, and special racing clothes protect the body. They also rely on safety technology on their motorcycle, such as good tires and brakes.

Imagine this ...

You are racing your motorcycle on a dirt race track. A cloud of dust is around you. You are in the lead, but another rider is almost beside you.

You speed up, just a little bit, to go faster around the last corner. You lean the bike over so it will go around the corner better.

You shouldn't have sped up. You're going too fast! The back wheel slips and slides. You fall, skidding on the dirt track.

You are sore and bruised, but you are not badly hurt!

Cycling Safely

Cyclists must wear a helmet to protect their head, and bright clothes, so they can be easily seen.

On a bicycle, good brakes help it to slow down and stop. A bicycle must also have reflective lights so it is easily seen at night, and in bad weather.

Bikes for All Ages!

A Preschool Bike (12 in wheels)
Designed for: 2–4 years old

A Girl's Bike (20 in wheels)
Designed for: 7–12 years old

A Starting-School Bike (12 in wheels)
Designed for: 5–7 years old

A Boy's Bike (20 in wheels)
Designed for: 7–12 years old

Racing Cyclists

Racing cyclists wear a special outfit that protects them and helps them go faster! Their clothes are very tight so the wind doesn't slow them down. Their gloves help them to hold on tightly. And their shoes have no laces, so they don't get caught in the wheels!

Which bike would you like to own?

A Girl's Bike (24 in wheels)
Designed for: 8–12 years old

A Lady's Bike (26 in wheels)
Designed for: 12 years old & over

A Boy's Bike (24 in wheels)
Designed for: 8–12 years old

A Man's Bike (26 in wheels)
Designed for: 12 years old & over

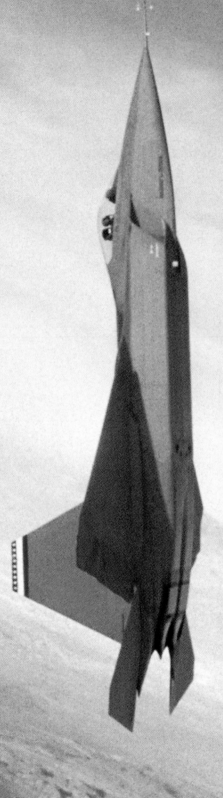

4. Escape!

Imagine this ...

You're flying in a jet fighter.
You're zooming upward at
hundreds of miles an hour.

Suddenly, a loud warning sound booms through your jet fighter. A flashing red light warns you of danger. Your computer screens tell you there's something wrong with your engine. You have three seconds to escape!

You hit a red button in front of you. Your ejector seat flings you out of the jet fighter. High above the ground, your parachute opens. Safety technology has helped you to escape speedily and safely from a very unsafe situation!

Aircraft Seat Belts

Whenever people travel in a plane, they must wear a seat belt. Seat belts protect passengers by holding them firmly in their seat.

If a plane flies into turbulence, it may drop suddenly. If people didn't wear seat belts, they might hit the roof of the plane.

What Is Turbulence?

High in the air, there are strong currents of wind. Sometimes these currents of wind move in different directions. This is called turbulence. If the plane flies into turbulence, you can have a bumpy ride!

Escaping Aircraft

Of course, not every aircraft has an ejector seat! To help people escape quickly from an aircraft, escape slides below the doors unroll and fill with air. People can slide down to safety. Under every seat, there is also a life jacket to wear.

Lifeboats, Life Rafts, and Life Jackets

At sea, lifeboats have saved many lives by helping people escape danger on ships. All ships and large boats must have enough lifeboats to carry all passengers and crew.

Ships and smaller boats may also carry life rafts. Like air bags, they fill up with air to stay afloat.

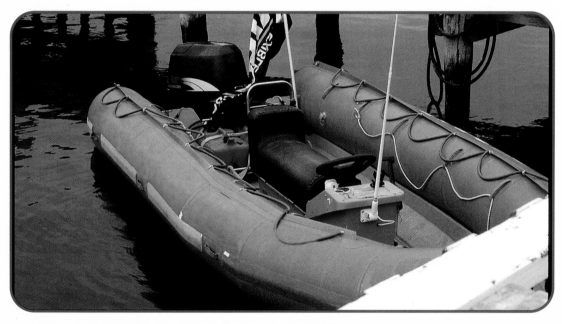

All ships and boats should have enough life jackets for everyone on board. On smaller boats, life jackets should be worn at all times. If someone falls overboard, they keep them afloat until help arrives.

Meet A Flight Team Pilot

Flight Lieutenant Joanne Mein

What Is a Flight Team? A Flight Team is a group of experienced display pilots. They fly their aircraft in formation at flying shows around the country. They also work as flying instructors.

Who Is Joanne Mein? Joanne is a member of a Flight Team.

How Can Flight Teams Fly Safely?

1. Their training includes many flights with the team leader. The team leader is very experienced in formation maneuvers.

2. Their formation maneuvers are practiced over and over again until they are perfect.

3. When the Flight Teams are flying in shows, only the team leader can tell the others when to change the formation. It is much safer when only one person is in charge.

5. Extreme Sports

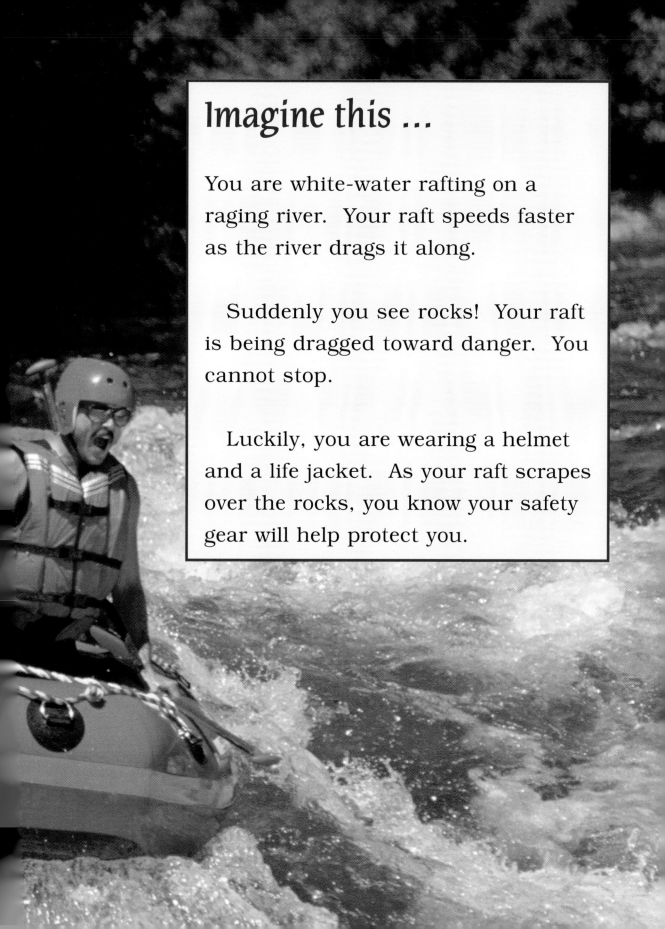

Imagine this ...

You are white-water rafting on a raging river. Your raft speeds faster as the river drags it along.

Suddenly you see rocks! Your raft is being dragged toward danger. You cannot stop.

Luckily, you are wearing a helmet and a life jacket. As your raft scrapes over the rocks, you know your safety gear will help protect you.

Of course, we may not want to go white-water rafting. But there are many other sports that are action-packed and extreme! In every sport, people need to wear safety gear to stay safe and have fun!

Snow Skiing

Snow skiers wear special padded suits that protect them if they fall, and keep them warm at the same time! They also wear thick gloves, goggles, boots and a hat. If they want to ski in a race or in a dangerous situation they wear a helmet too.

Goggles

Snow skiers need to wear goggles for two main reasons:

1. To protect their eyes from splashing snow and dirt.

2. To protect their eyes from the sun — just like sunglasses!

   If the sun is shining brightly, the sunlight reflects off the snow and can hurt people's eyes. Skiers can even get sunburned!

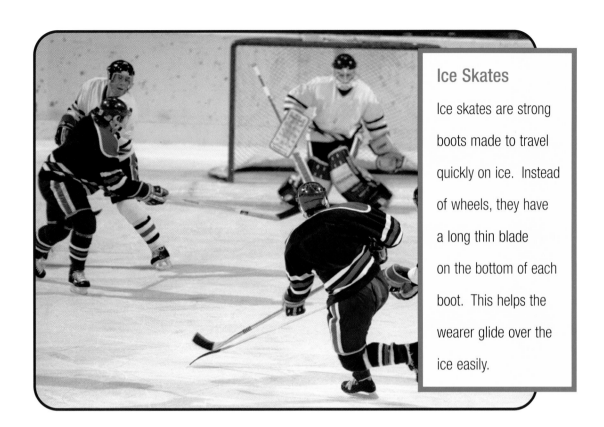

Ice Skates

Ice skates are strong boots made to travel quickly on ice. Instead of wheels, they have a long thin blade on the bottom of each boot. This helps the wearer glide over the ice easily.

Ice Hockey

Ice hockey is a very fast sport, using a hockey stick and a puck (a hard, flat disc). Players need to wear padded clothing to protect themselves if they fall over on the hard ice or if they are hit by a stick or the puck. Each player also wears ice skates, a helmet, and a mouth guard. The goalkeepers even wear face masks! All of this safety technology has been made to help ice hockey players play quickly and safely.

6. Speedy Fun

Imagine this ...

You're speeding around the track in your bumper car. You have been told to drive safely. All around you, bumper cars are bumping and crashing into each other. Suddenly you can see someone's car speeding toward you. You're going to be bumped, and bumped hard! What can you do?

Safety In Bumper Cars

Bumper cars are safe and fun to bump and crash around the track. Here are five reasons:

1. Everyone must wear a seat belt.

2. Everyone must drive in the same direction.

3. Bumper cars have wide, large rubber bumpers all around them (so they bounce back if they crash).

4. Bumper cars are built out of very strong metal.

5. There is always a supervisor at the bumper car track to make sure people are driving safely.

In-Line Skating

In-line skating can be fast and fun if you practice in a safe place first. In-line skaters can use sidewalks, bicycle tracks, and even driveways!

To protect themselves, in-line skaters need to wear special gear. They must wear a helmet, gloves, elbow pads and knee pads, to protect themselves if they fall. Their skates are laced and strapped on tightly. The skates' thin wheels are made to move very fast!

Have Fun But Stay Safe!

Just remember ... whatever you choose to do in sports, activities, or when traveling, you can have fun if you follow some simple rules. So before you complain about wearing a seat belt in your car, or having to wear a helmet when riding a bike, or maybe even wearing floaties in the pool, think about how safety technology could save your life and many others!

Index

air bags 12, 21
bicycles 16–17, 31
brakes 12, 15, 16
bumper cars 28–29
cars 4–13
drag racing 6
dummy 9, 13
ejector seat 19, 20
fireproof clothes 7
Flight Team 22
gloves 7, 15, 30
goggles 26
helmet 5, 7, 15, 16, 25, 26, 30, 31
ice hockey 27
ice skates 27
in-line skating 30
lifeboats 21
life jackets 20–21, 25
life rafts 21
motorcycles 14–15
parachute 6–7, 19
puck 27
race car 4–7
reflective lights 16
safety clothes 5, 15
safety seat 11
safety test 9, 13
seat belt 10–11, 20, 29, 31
skiing 26
steel frames 13
steering wheel 12
sun glare 26
tire 5, 15
turbulence 20
wheels 12
white-water rafting 25–26

Bookweb Links

Read more Bookweb 3 books about
action and travel!

Ready for Take-Off! — Nonfiction

The Abominable Snowman — Fiction

Same Idea, Different Year — Fiction

Hugo and Splot — Fiction

Key To Bookweb
Fact Boxes

☐ Arts

☐ Health

☐ Science

☐ Social Studies

☐ Technology